This journal belongs to:

DEDICATION

This Kindness Journal is dedicated to all the people out there who love to track their good deeds and want to document their findings in the process.

You are my inspiration for producing books and I'm honored to be a part of keeping all of your Acts Of Kindness notes and records organized.

This journal notebook will help you record your details about tracking your kindness.

Thoughtfully put together with these sections to record:
Date & Time, Recipient, What I Did, Why I Did It, How They Responded, How It Made Me Feel, I Am Inspired To, An Act Of Kindness I Saw Today, & Notes.

HOW TO USE THIS BOOK

The purpose of this book is to keep all of your Acts Of Kindness notes all in one place. It will help keep you organized.

This Kindness Journal will allow you to accurately document every detail about your Acts Of Kindness. It's a great way to chart your course through tracking your kindness.

Here are examples of the prompts for you to fill in and write about your experience in this book:

1. **Date, Time** - Write the date & time of your kindness act.

2. **Recipient** - Record to whom your act of kindness was directed to.

3. **What I Did** - Log your act of kindness.

4. **Why I Did It** - Write your reason for the act of kindness.

5. **How They Responded** - Record how the recipient responded.

6. **How It Made Me Feel** - Log how the act your performed made you feel.

7. **I Am Inspired To** - What did the act of kindness inspire you to do.

8. **An Act Of Kindness I Saw Today** - What act of kindness did someone else do that you saw.

9. **Notes** - For any important information you wish to record such as your gratitude, set goals, favorite Bible verse, thoughts, quotes, any idea, blessings, words of wisdom, lists.

Recipient:

What I did:

Why I did it:

How they responded:

How it made me feel:

I am inspired to:

An act of kindness I saw today:

Additional Notes or Drawings:

DATE

TIME

Recipient:

What I did:

Why I did it:

How they responded:

How it made me feel:

I am inspired to:

An act of kindness I saw today:

Additional Notes or Drawings:

DATE

TIME

Recipient:

What I did:

Why I did it:

How they responded:

How it made me feel:

I am inspired to:

An act of kindness I saw today:

Additional Notes or Drawings:

Recipient:

What I did:

Why I did it:

How they responded:

How it made me feel:

I am inspired to:

An act of kindness I saw today:

Additional Notes or Drawings:

DATE

TIME

Recipient:

What I did:

Why I did it:

How they responded:

How it made me feel:

I am inspired to:

An act of kindness I saw today:

Additional Notes or Drawings:

Recipient:

What I did:

Why I did it:

How they responded:

How it made me feel:

I am inspired to:

An act of kindness I saw today:

Additional Notes or Drawings:

Recipient:

What I did:

Why I did it:

How they responded:

How it made me feel:

I am inspired to:

An act of kindness I saw today:

Additional Notes or Drawings:

DATE

TIME

Recipient:

What I did:

Why I did it:

How they responded:

How it made me feel:

I am inspired to:

An act of kindness I saw today:

Additional Notes or Drawings:

Recipient:

What I did:

Why I did it:

How they responded:

How it made me feel:

I am inspired to:

An act of kindness I saw today:

Additional Notes or Drawings:

DATE

TIME

Recipient:

What I did:

Why I did it:

How they responded:

How it made me feel:

I am inspired to:

An act of kindness I saw today:

Additional Notes or Drawings:

DATE

TIME

Recipient:

What I did:

Why I did it:

How they responded:

How it made me feel:

I am inspired to:

An act of kindness I saw today:

Additional Notes or Drawings:

DATE

TIME

Recipient:

What I did:

Why I did it:

How they responded:

How it made me feel:

I am inspired to:

An act of kindness I saw today:

Additional Notes or Drawings:

Recipient:

What I did:

Why I did it:

How they responded:

How it made me feel:

I am inspired to:

An act of kindness I saw today:

Additional Notes or Drawings:

Recipient:

What I did:

Why I did it:

How they responded:

How it made me feel:

I am inspired to:

An act of kindness I saw today:

Additional Notes or Drawings:

Recipient:

What I did:

Why I did it:

How they responded:

How it made me feel:

I am inspired to:

An act of kindness I saw today:

Additional Notes or Drawings:

Recipient:

What I did:

Why I did it:

How they responded:

How it made me feel:

I am inspired to:

An act of kindness I saw today:

Additional Notes or Drawings:

Recipient:

What I did:

Why I did it:

How they responded:

How it made me feel:

I am inspired to:

An act of kindness I saw today:

Additional Notes or Drawings:

Recipient:

What I did:

Why I did it:

How they responded:

How it made me feel:

I am inspired to:

An act of kindness I saw today:

Additional Notes or Drawings:

DATE

TIME

Recipient:

What I did:

Why I did it:

How they responded:

How it made me feel:

I am inspired to:

An act of kindness I saw today:

Additional Notes or Drawings:

DATE

TIME

Recipient:

What I did:

Why I did it:

How they responded:

How it made me feel:

I am inspired to:

An act of kindness I saw today:

Additional Notes or Drawings:

Recipient:

What I did:

Why I did it:

How they responded:

How it made me feel:

I am inspired to:

An act of kindness I saw today:

Additional Notes or Drawings:

Recipient:

What I did:

Why I did it:

How they responded:

How it made me feel:

I am inspired to:

An act of kindness I saw today:

Additional Notes or Drawings:

Recipient:

What I did:

Why I did it:

How they responded:

How it made me feel:

I am inspired to:

An act of kindness I saw today:

Additional Notes or Drawings:

DATE

TIME

Recipient:

What I did:

Why I did it:

How they responded:

How it made me feel:

I am inspired to:

An act of kindness I saw today:

Additional Notes or Drawings:

Recipient:

What I did:

Why I did it:

How they responded:

How it made me feel:

I am inspired to:

An act of kindness I saw today:

Additional Notes or Drawings:

DATE

TIME

Recipient:

What I did:

DATE

TIME

Why I did it:

How they responded:

How it made me feel:

I am inspired to:

An act of kindness I saw today:

Additional Notes or Drawings:

Recipient:

What I did:

Why I did it:

How they responded:

How it made me feel:

I am inspired to:

An act of kindness I saw today:

Additional Notes or Drawings:

Recipient:

What I did:

Why I did it:

How they responded:

How it made me feel:

I am inspired to:

An act of kindness I saw today:

Additional Notes or Drawings:

Recipient:

What I did:

Why I did it:

How they responded:

How it made me feel:

I am inspired to:

An act of kindness I saw today:

Additional Notes or Drawings:

DATE

TIME

Recipient: _____

What I did: _____

Why I did it: _____

How they responded: _____

How it made me feel: _____

I am inspired to: _____

An act of kindness I saw today: _____

Additional Notes or Drawings:

Recipient:

What I did:

Why I did it:

How they responded:

How it made me feel:

I am inspired to:

An act of kindness I saw today:

Additional Notes or Drawings:

DATE

TIME

Recipient:

What I did:

Why I did it:

How they responded:

How it made me feel:

I am inspired to:

An act of kindness I saw today:

Additional Notes or Drawings:

Recipient:

What I did:

Why I did it:

How they responded:

How it made me feel:

I am inspired to:

An act of kindness I saw today:

Additional Notes or Drawings:

DATE

TIME

Recipient:

What I did:

Why I did it:

How they responded:

How it made me feel:

I am inspired to:

An act of kindness I saw today:

Additional Notes or Drawings:

Recipient:

What I did:

Why I did it:

How they responded:

How it made me feel:

I am inspired to:

An act of kindness I saw today:

Additional Notes or Drawings:

Recipient:

What I did:

Why I did it:

How they responded:

How it made me feel:

I am inspired to:

An act of kindness I saw today:

Additional Notes or Drawings:

DATE

TIME

Recipient:

What I did:

Why I did it:

How they responded:

How it made me feel:

I am inspired to:

An act of kindness I saw today:

Additional Notes or Drawings:

Recipient:

What I did:

Why I did it:

How they responded:

How it made me feel:

I am inspired to:

An act of kindness I saw today:

Additional Notes or Drawings:

Recipient:

What I did:

Why I did it:

How they responded:

How it made me feel:

I am inspired to:

An act of kindness I saw today:

Additional Notes or Drawings:

DATE

TIME

Recipient:

What I did:

Why I did it:

How they responded:

How it made me feel:

I am inspired to:

An act of kindness I saw today:

Additional Notes or Drawings:

DATE

TIME

Recipient:

What I did:

Why I did it:

How they responded:

How it made me feel:

I am inspired to:

An act of kindness I saw today:

Additional Notes or Drawings:

DATE

TIME

Recipient:

What I did:

Why I did it:

How they responded:

How it made me feel:

I am inspired to:

An act of kindness I saw today:

Additional Notes or Drawings:

Recipient:

What I did:

Why I did it:

How they responded:

How it made me feel:

I am inspired to:

An act of kindness I saw today:

Additional Notes or Drawings:

DATE

TIME

Recipient:

What I did:

Why I did it:

How they responded:

How it made me feel:

I am inspired to:

An act of kindness I saw today:

Additional Notes or Drawings:

Recipient:

What I did:

Why I did it:

How they responded:

How it made me feel:

I am inspired to:

An act of kindness I saw today:

Additional Notes or Drawings:

Recipient:

What I did:

Why I did it:

How they responded:

How it made me feel:

I am inspired to:

An act of kindness I saw today:

Additional Notes or Drawings:

DATE

TIME

Recipient:

What I did:

Why I did it:

How they responded:

How it made me feel:

I am inspired to:

An act of kindness I saw today:

Additional Notes or Drawings:

DATE

TIME

Recipient:

What I did:

Why I did it:

How they responded:

How it made me feel:

I am inspired to:

An act of kindness I saw today:

Additional Notes or Drawings:

DATE

TIME

Recipient:

What I did:

Why I did it:

How they responded:

How it made me feel:

I am inspired to:

An act of kindness I saw today:

Additional Notes or Drawings:

DATE

TIME

Recipient:

What I did:

Why I did it:

How they responded:

How it made me feel:

I am inspired to:

An act of kindness I saw today:

Additional Notes or Drawings:

Recipient:

What I did:

Why I did it:

How they responded:

How it made me feel:

I am inspired to:

An act of kindness I saw today:

Additional Notes or Drawings:

DATE

TIME

Recipient:

What I did:

Why I did it:

How they responded:

How it made me feel:

I am inspired to:

An act of kindness I saw today:

Additional Notes or Drawings:

Recipient:

What I did:

Why I did it:

How they responded:

How it made me feel:

I am inspired to:

An act of kindness I saw today:

Additional Notes or Drawings:

DATE

TIME

Recipient:

What I did:

Why I did it:

How they responded:

How it made me feel:

I am inspired to:

An act of kindness I saw today:

Additional Notes or Drawings:

Recipient:

What I did:

Why I did it:

How they responded:

How it made me feel:

I am inspired to:

An act of kindness I saw today:

Additional Notes or Drawings:

Recipient: _____

What I did: _____

Why I did it: _____

How they responded: _____

How it made me feel: _____

I am inspired to: _____

An act of kindness I saw today: _____

Additional Notes or Drawings:

Recipient:

What I did:

Why I did it:

How they responded:

How it made me feel:

I am inspired to:

An act of kindness I saw today:

Additional Notes or Drawings:

DATE

TIME

Recipient:

What I did:

Why I did it:

How they responded:

How it made me feel:

I am inspired to:

An act of kindness I saw today:

Additional Notes or Drawings:

DATE

TIME

Recipient:

What I did:

Why I did it:

How they responded:

How it made me feel:

I am inspired to:

An act of kindness I saw today:

Additional Notes or Drawings:

DATE

TIME

Recipient:

What I did:

Why I did it:

How they responded:

How it made me feel:

I am inspired to:

An act of kindness I saw today:

Additional Notes or Drawings:

DATE

TIME

Recipient:

What I did:

Why I did it:

How they responded:

How it made me feel:

I am inspired to:

An act of kindness I saw today:

Additional Notes or Drawings:

DATE

TIME

Recipient:

What I did:

Why I did it:

How they responded:

How it made me feel:

I am inspired to:

An act of kindness I saw today:

Additional Notes or Drawings:

DATE

TIME

Recipient:

What I did:

Why I did it:

How they responded:

How it made me feel:

I am inspired to:

An act of kindness I saw today:

Additional Notes or Drawings:

Recipient:

What I did:

Why I did it:

How they responded:

How it made me feel:

I am inspired to:

An act of kindness I saw today:

Additional Notes or Drawings:

Recipient:

What I did:

Why I did it:

How they responded:

How it made me feel:

I am inspired to:

An act of kindness I saw today:

Additional Notes or Drawings:

DATE

TIME

Recipient:

What I did:

Why I did it:

How they responded:

How it made me feel:

I am inspired to:

An act of kindness I saw today:

Additional Notes or Drawings:

DATE

TIME

Recipient:

What I did:

Why I did it:

How they responded:

How it made me feel:

I am inspired to:

An act of kindness I saw today:

Additional Notes or Drawings:

DATE

TIME

Recipient:

What I did:

Why I did it:

How they responded:

How it made me feel:

I am inspired to:

An act of kindness I saw today:

Additional Notes or Drawings:

Recipient:

What I did:

Why I did it:

How they responded:

How it made me feel:

I am inspired to:

An act of kindness I saw today:

Additional Notes or Drawings:

DATE

TIME

Recipient:

What I did:

Why I did it:

How they responded:

How it made me feel:

I am inspired to:

An act of kindness I saw today:

Additional Notes or Drawings:

Recipient:

What I did:

Why I did it:

How they responded:

How it made me feel:

I am inspired to:

An act of kindness I saw today:

Additional Notes or Drawings:

Recipient:

What I did:

Why I did it:

How they responded:

How it made me feel:

I am inspired to:

An act of kindness I saw today:

Additional Notes or Drawings:

DATE

TIME

Recipient:

What I did:

Why I did it:

How they responded:

How it made me feel:

I am inspired to:

An act of kindness I saw today:

Additional Notes or Drawings:

Recipient:

What I did:

Why I did it:

How they responded:

How it made me feel:

I am inspired to:

An act of kindness I saw today:

Additional Notes or Drawings:

DATE

TIME

Recipient:

What I did:

Why I did it:

How they responded:

How it made me feel:

I am inspired to:

An act of kindness I saw today:

Additional Notes or Drawings:

DATE

TIME

Recipient:

What I did:

Why I did it:

How they responded:

How it made me feel:

I am inspired to:

An act of kindness I saw today:

Additional Notes or Drawings:

DATE

TIME

Recipient:

What I did:

Why I did it:

How they responded:

How it made me feel:

I am inspired to:

An act of kindness I saw today:

Additional Notes or Drawings:

DATE

TIME

Recipient:

What I did:

Why I did it:

How they responded:

How it made me feel:

I am inspired to:

An act of kindness I saw today:

Additional Notes or Drawings:

DATE

TIME

Recipient:

What I did:

Why I did it:

How they responded:

How it made me feel:

I am inspired to:

An act of kindness I saw today:

Additional Notes or Drawings:

DATE

TIME

Recipient:

What I did:

Why I did it:

How they responded:

How it made me feel:

I am inspired to:

An act of kindness I saw today:

Additional Notes or Drawings:

DATE

TIME

Recipient:

What I did:

Why I did it:

How they responded:

How it made me feel:

I am inspired to:

An act of kindness I saw today:

Additional Notes or Drawings:

DATE

TIME

Recipient:

What I did:

Why I did it:

How they responded:

How it made me feel:

I am inspired to:

An act of kindness I saw today:

Additional Notes or Drawings:

Recipient:

What I did:

Why I did it:

How they responded:

How it made me feel:

I am inspired to:

An act of kindness I saw today:

Additional Notes or Drawings:

DATE

TIME

Recipient:

What I did:

Why I did it:

How they responded:

How it made me feel:

I am inspired to:

An act of kindness I saw today:

Additional Notes or Drawings:

DATE

TIME

Recipient:

What I did:

Why I did it:

How they responded:

How it made me feel:

I am inspired to:

An act of kindness I saw today:

Additional Notes or Drawings:

Recipient: _____

What I did: _____

Why I did it: _____

How they responded: _____

How it made me feel: _____

I am inspired to: _____

An act of kindness I saw today: _____

Additional Notes or Drawings:

Recipient:

What I did:

Why I did it:

How they responded:

How it made me feel:

I am inspired to:

An act of kindness I saw today:

Additional Notes or Drawings:

Recipient: _____

What I did: _____

Why I did it: _____

How they responded: _____

How it made me feel: _____

I am inspired to: _____

An act of kindness I saw today: _____

Additional Notes or Drawings:

Recipient:

What I did:

Why I did it:

How they responded:

How it made me feel:

I am inspired to:

An act of kindness I saw today:

Additional Notes or Drawings:

Recipient:

What I did:

Why I did it:

How they responded:

How it made me feel:

I am inspired to:

An act of kindness I saw today:

Additional Notes or Drawings:

Recipient:

What I did:

Why I did it:

How they responded:

How it made me feel:

I am inspired to:

An act of kindness I saw today:

Additional Notes or Drawings:

DATE

TIME

Recipient:

What I did:

Why I did it:

How they responded:

How it made me feel:

I am inspired to:

An act of kindness I saw today:

Additional Notes or Drawings:

DATE

TIME

Recipient:

What I did:

Why I did it:

How they responded:

How it made me feel:

I am inspired to:

An act of kindness I saw today:

Additional Notes or Drawings:

Recipient:

What I did:

Why I did it:

How they responded:

How it made me feel:

I am inspired to:

An act of kindness I saw today:

Additional Notes or Drawings:

Recipient:

What I did:

Why I did it:

How they responded:

How it made me feel:

I am inspired to:

An act of kindness I saw today:

Additional Notes or Drawings:

Recipient:

What I did:

Why I did it:

How they responded:

How it made me feel:

I am inspired to:

An act of kindness I saw today:

Additional Notes or Drawings:

Recipient:

What I did:

Why I did it:

How they responded:

How it made me feel:

I am inspired to:

An act of kindness I saw today:

Additional Notes or Drawings:

DATE

TIME

Recipient:

What I did:

Why I did it:

How they responded:

How it made me feel:

I am inspired to:

An act of kindness I saw today:

Additional Notes or Drawings: